Spirit of Dogs
Adult Coloring Book

An Exploration of the Indomitable Spirit of Rescue Dogs

It's a Rescue Dog Life

DEDICATION

To all Rescue Dog lovers, big and small.
And to the Rescue Dogs that inspired it all: Jack and Ezra,
and their best friend: Chloe.

ACKNOWLEDGEMENT

Thank you to the following publications for the "spirit" component of these designs:

- Archie (Ward & Griffith, 1902, p. 150)
- Bailey (Washburn & Co & Henry G. Gilbert Nursery and Seed Trade Catalog Co, 1869, p. 53)
- Bella (Childs & Collection, 1914, p. 128)
- Bruno (Snyder, n.d.)
- Emma (Hooker, 1830-1833, p. 458)
- Ezra (Dodge, 1873, p. 93)
- Gracie (Ricci & Sara Anderson Galleries, Inc., 1915, p. 78)
- Heidi (Herbert, 1868, p. 293)
- Jack (Hood & Shepherd, 1881, p. 580)
- Jake (Figuier & Gillmore, 1869, p. 435)
- Lucky (Bass, 1900, p. 16)
- Max (W & Mulready, 1883, p. 20)
- Milo (Elton, 1854, p. 35)
- Molly (various, 1902, p. 506)
- Penny (The Craftsman, 1901, p. 374)
- Rusty (Ball, 1891, p. 235)
- Scout (Alpine Club London & Ball, 1859, p. 192)
- Simon (Kipling & Willeumier, 1895, p. 221)

Archie

Spirit of Dogs Adult Coloring Book

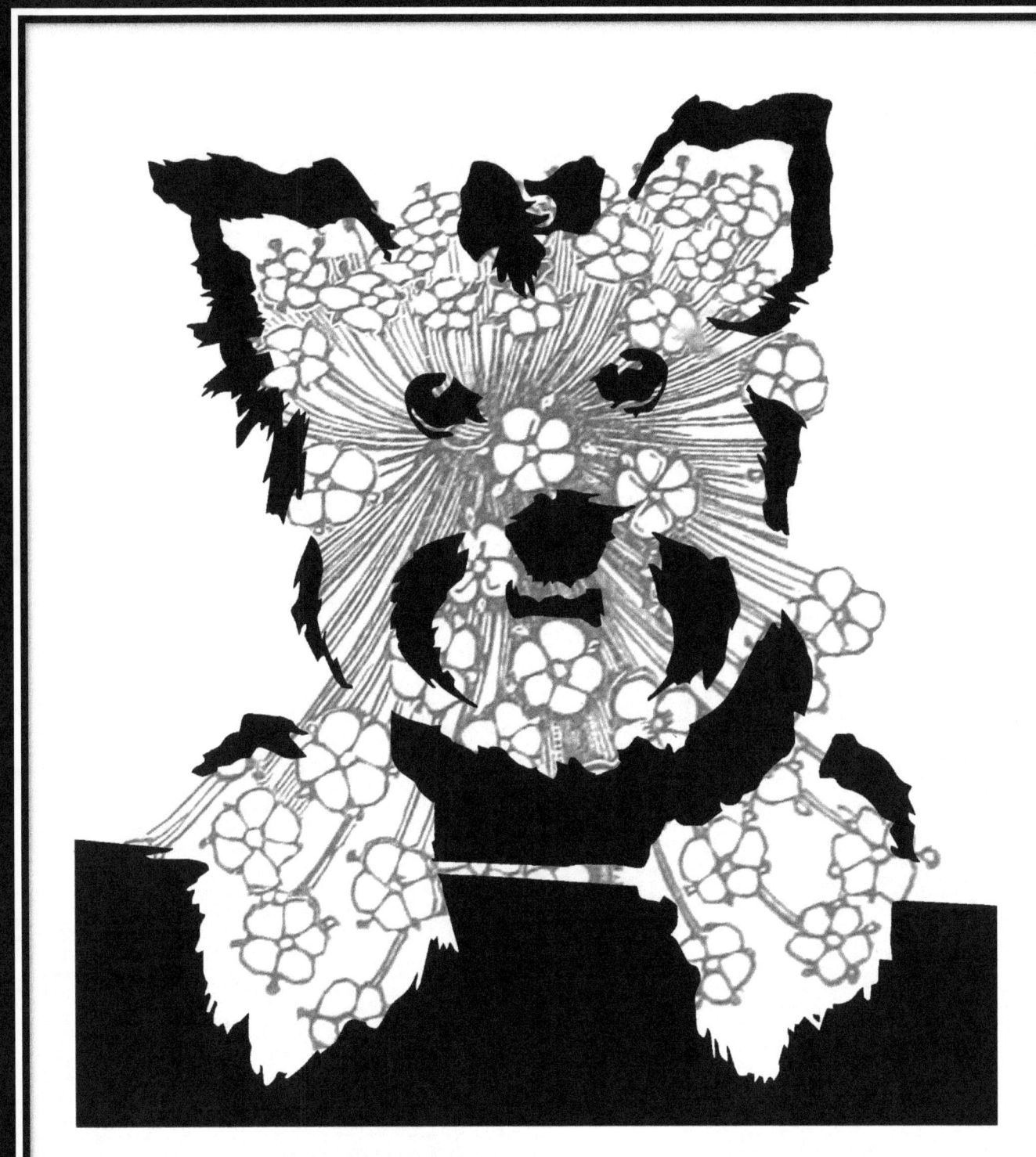

Bailey

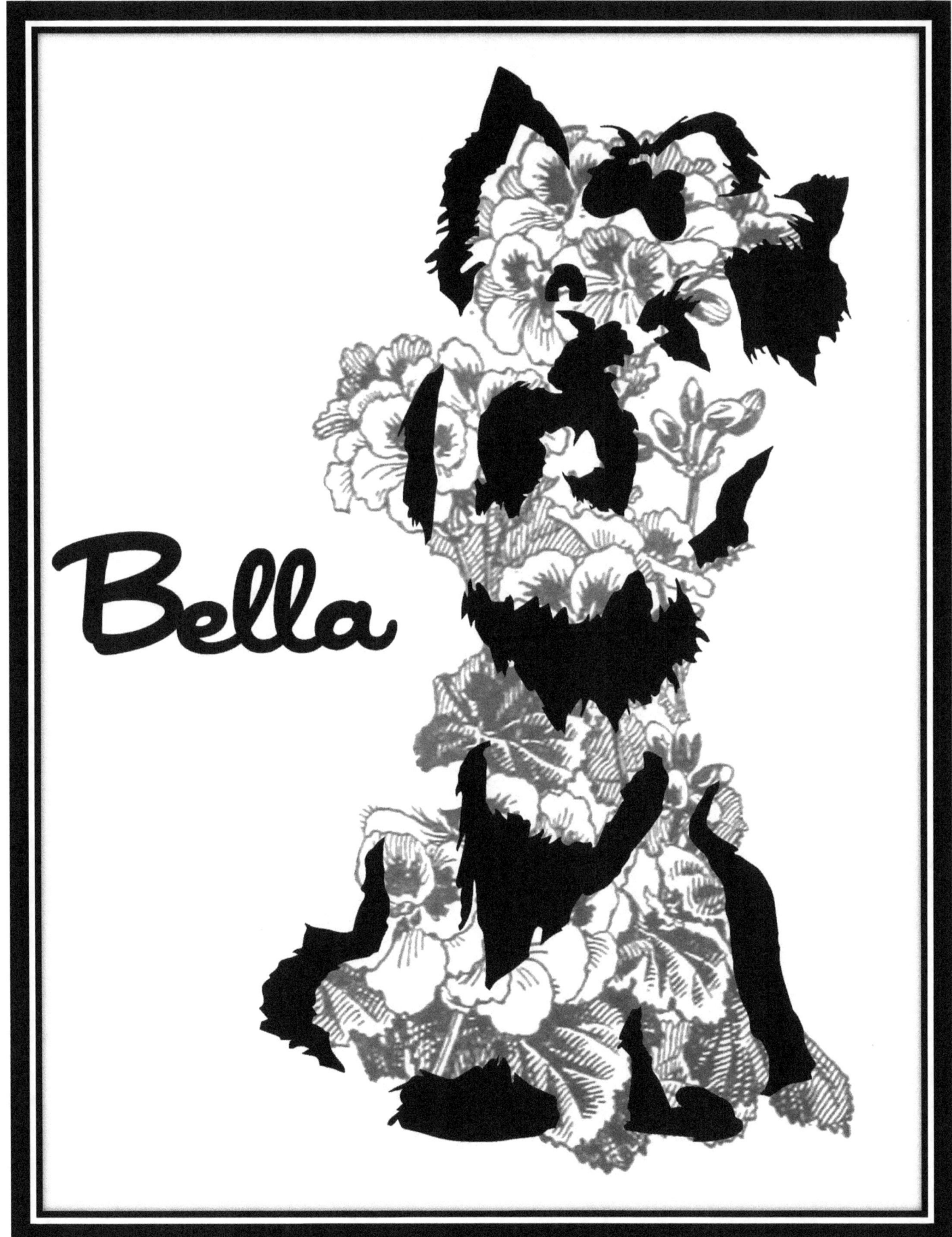

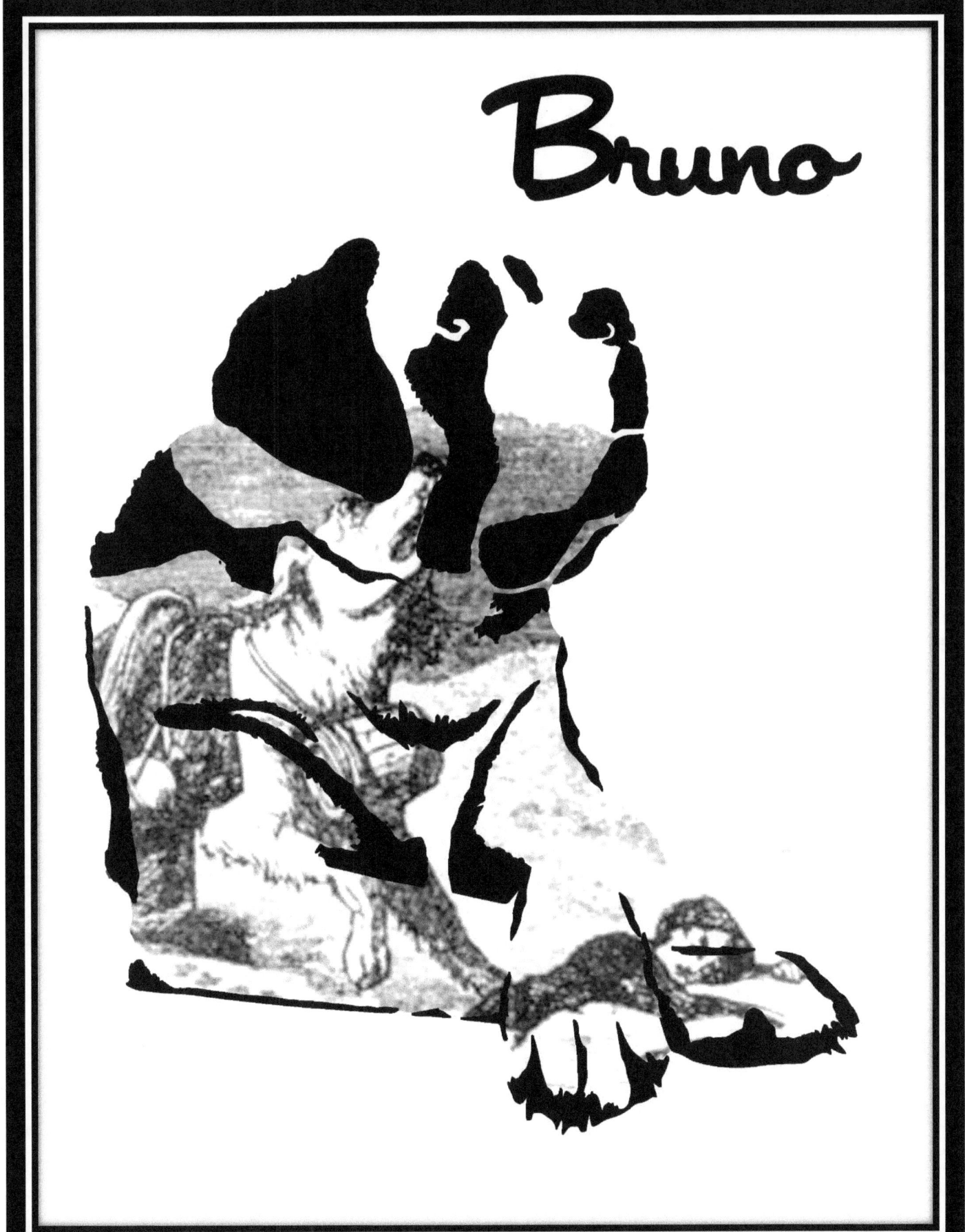

Bruno

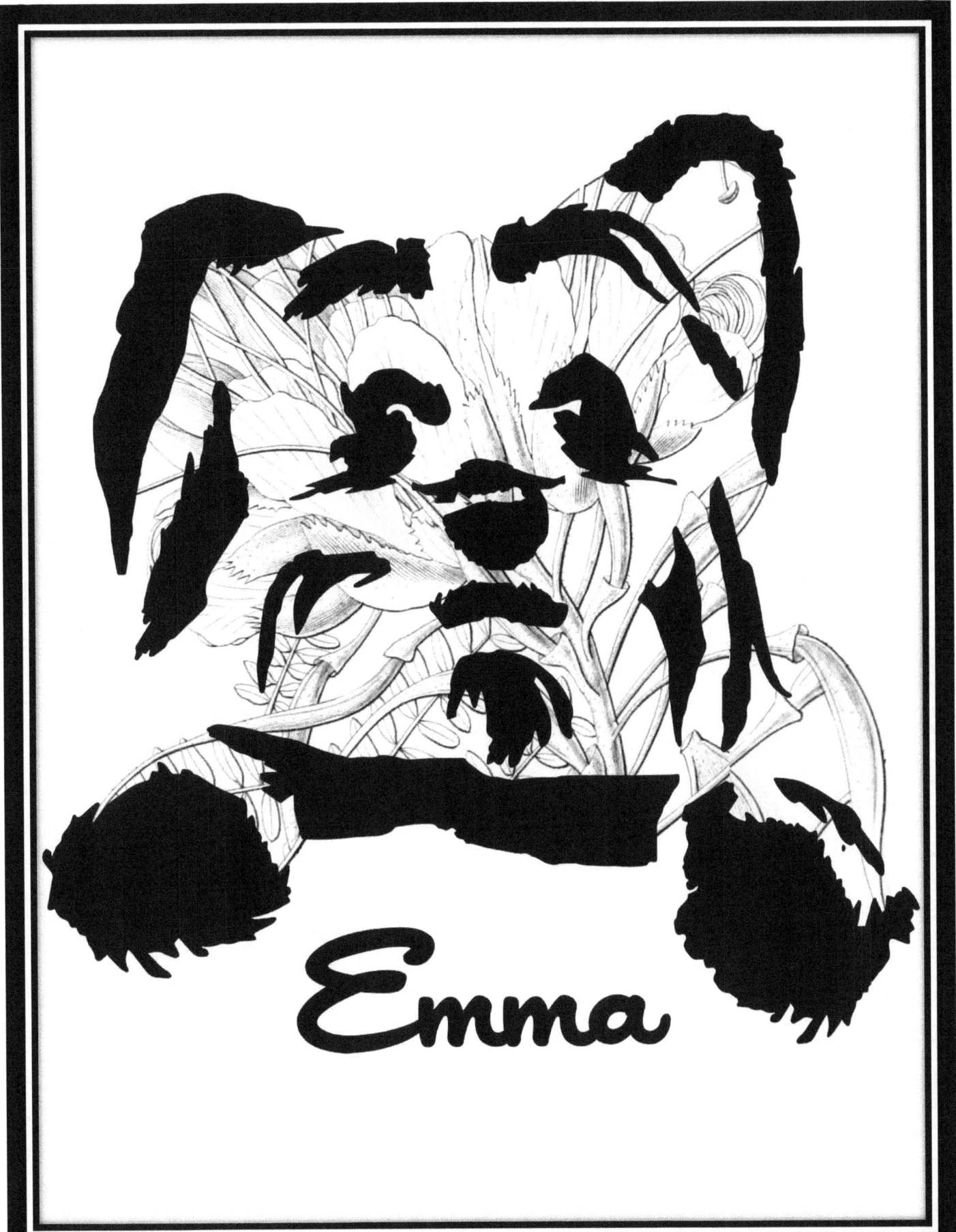

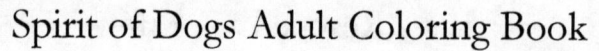

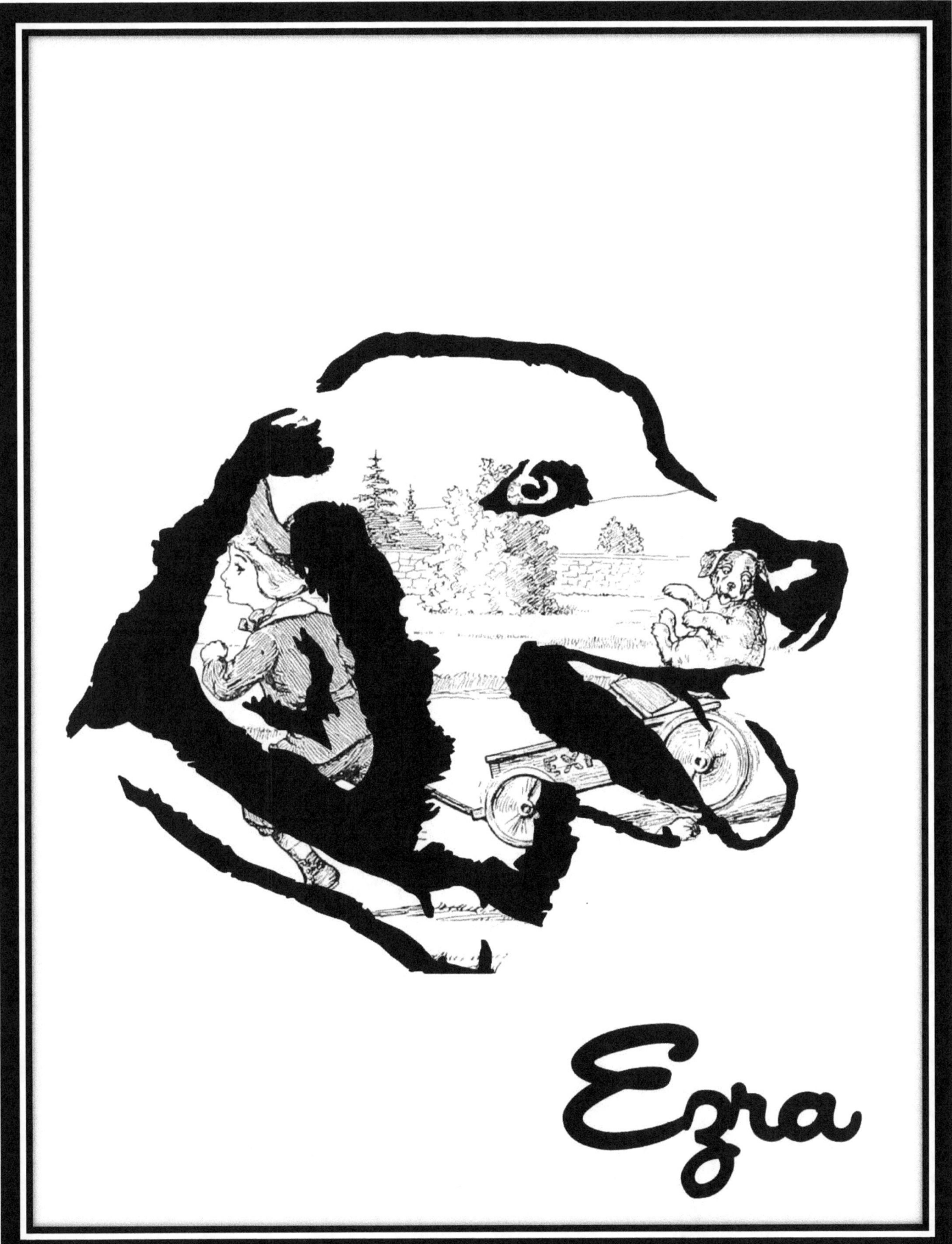

Ezra

Gracie

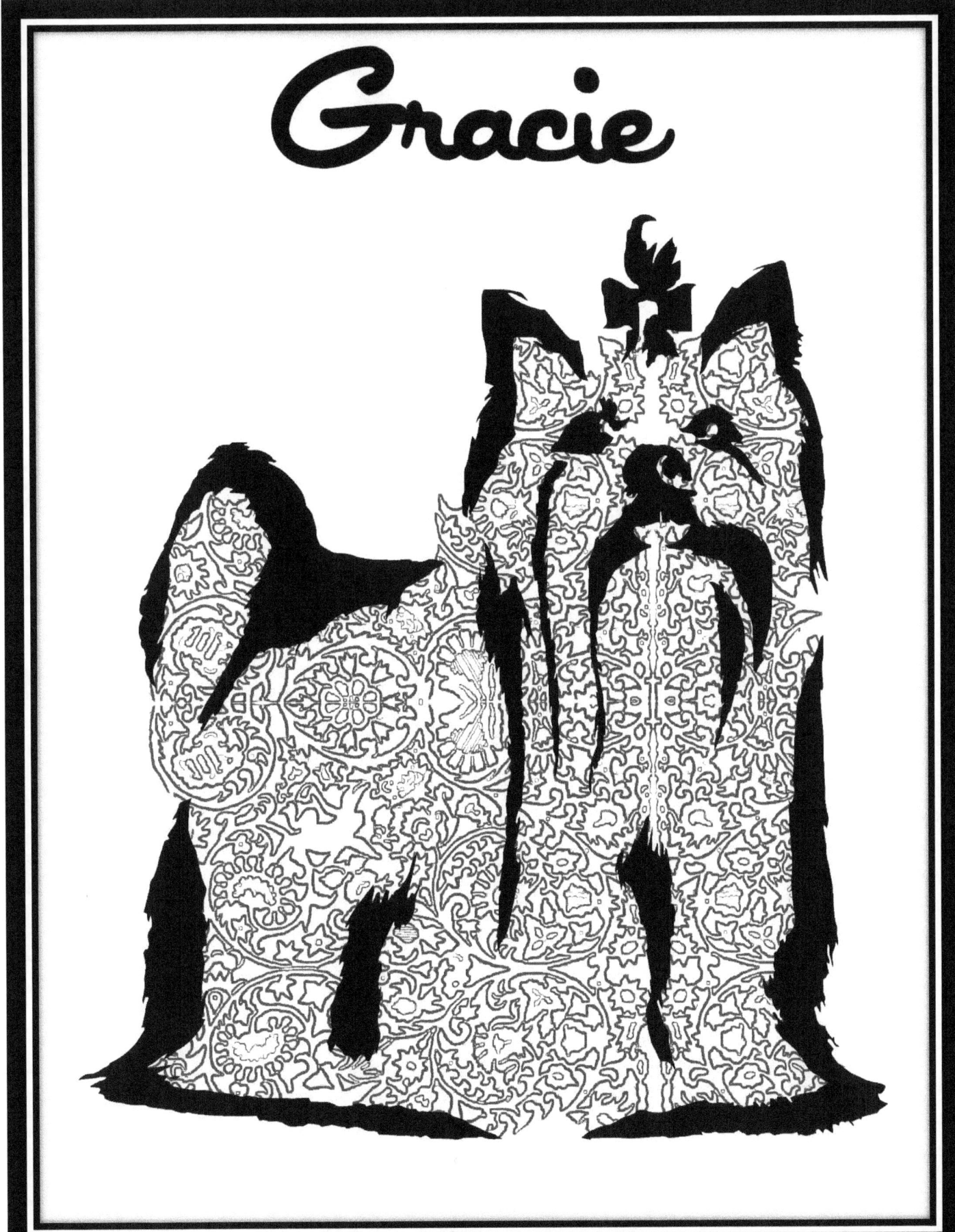

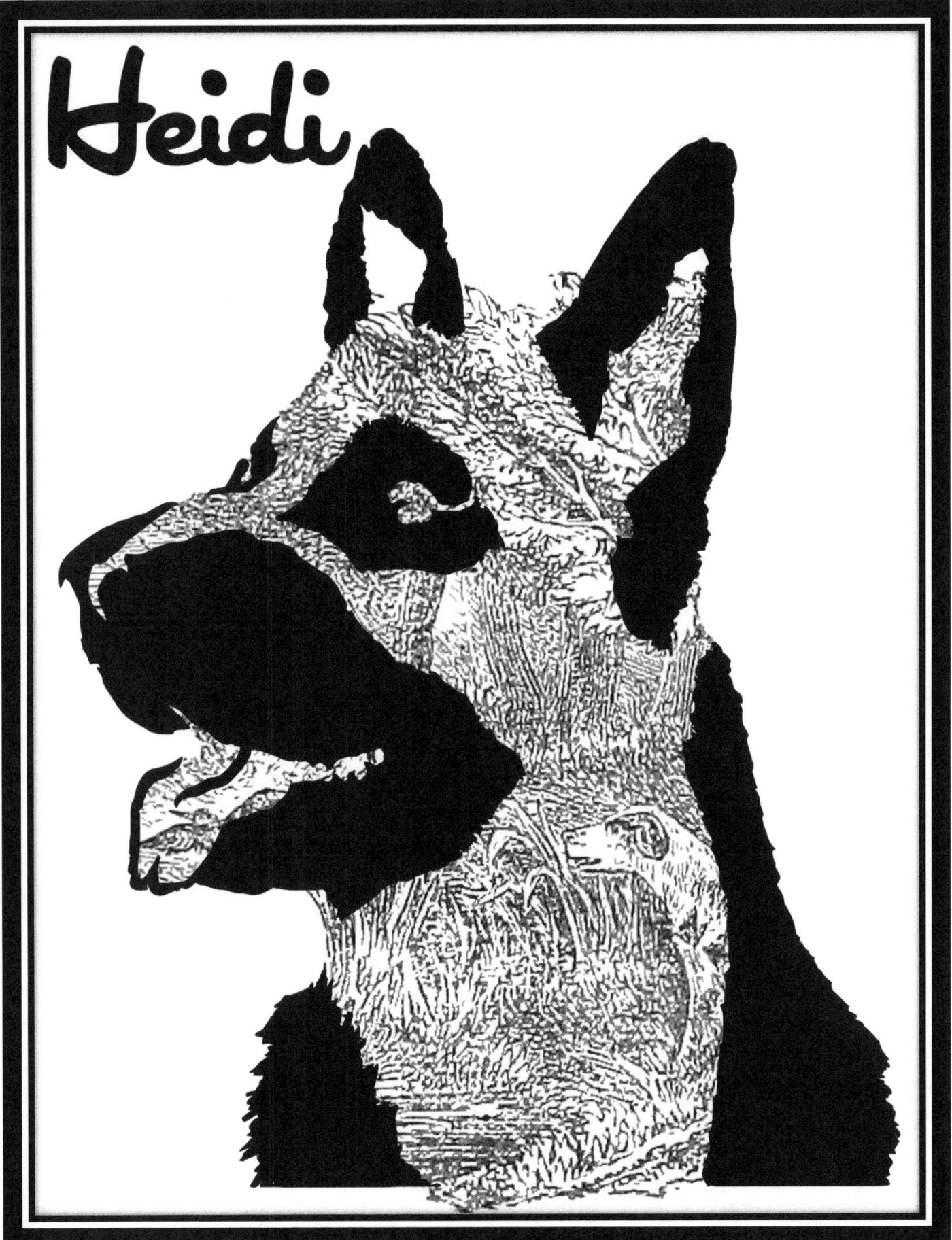

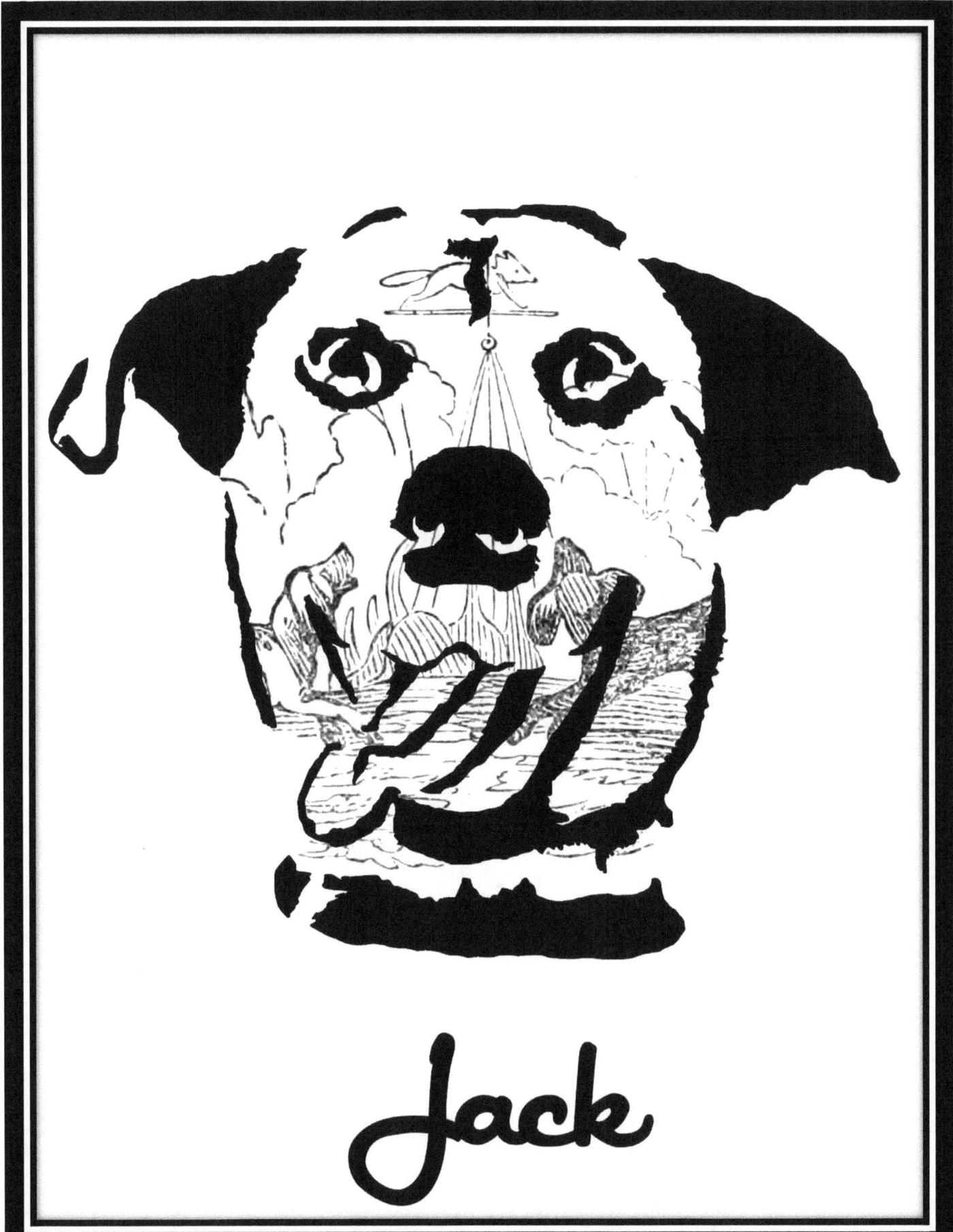

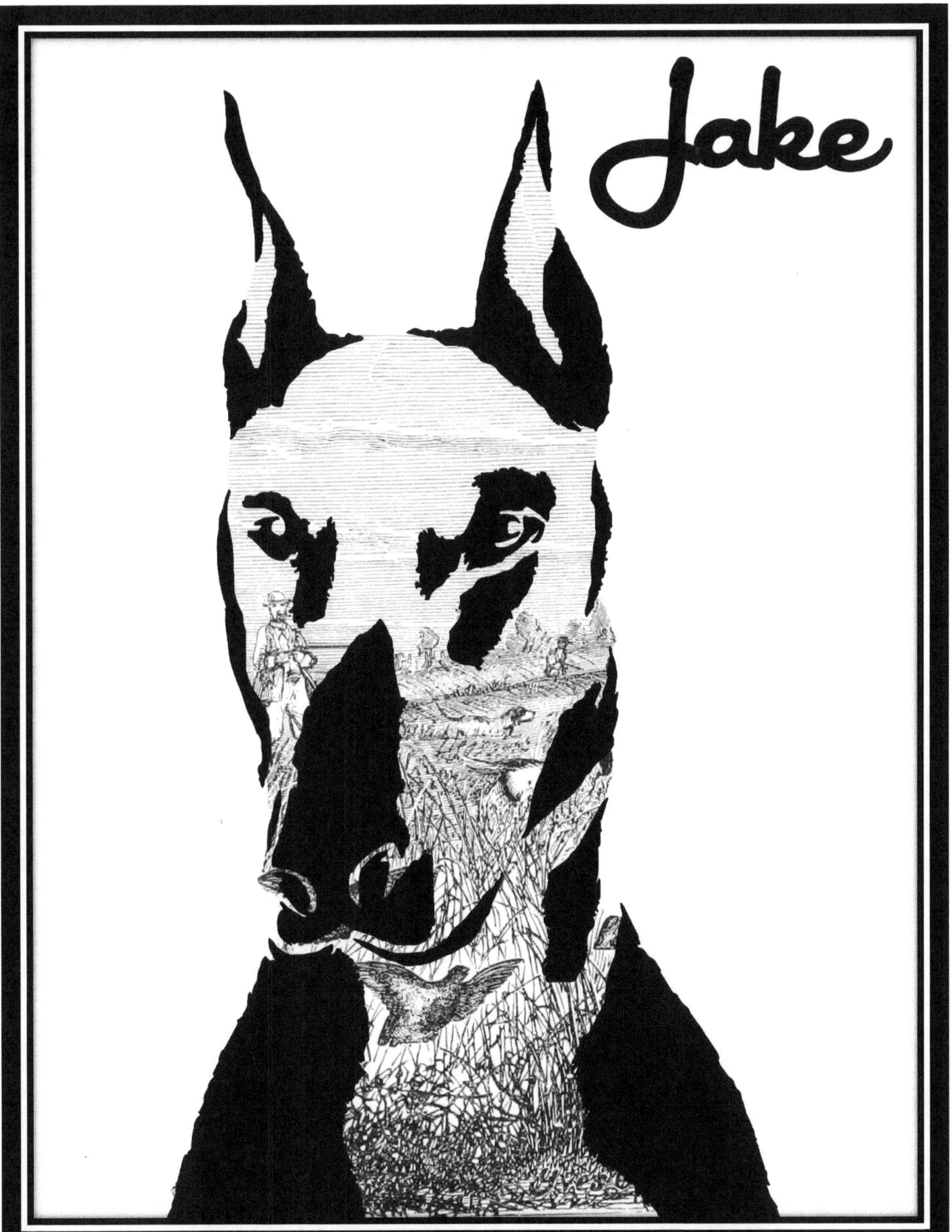

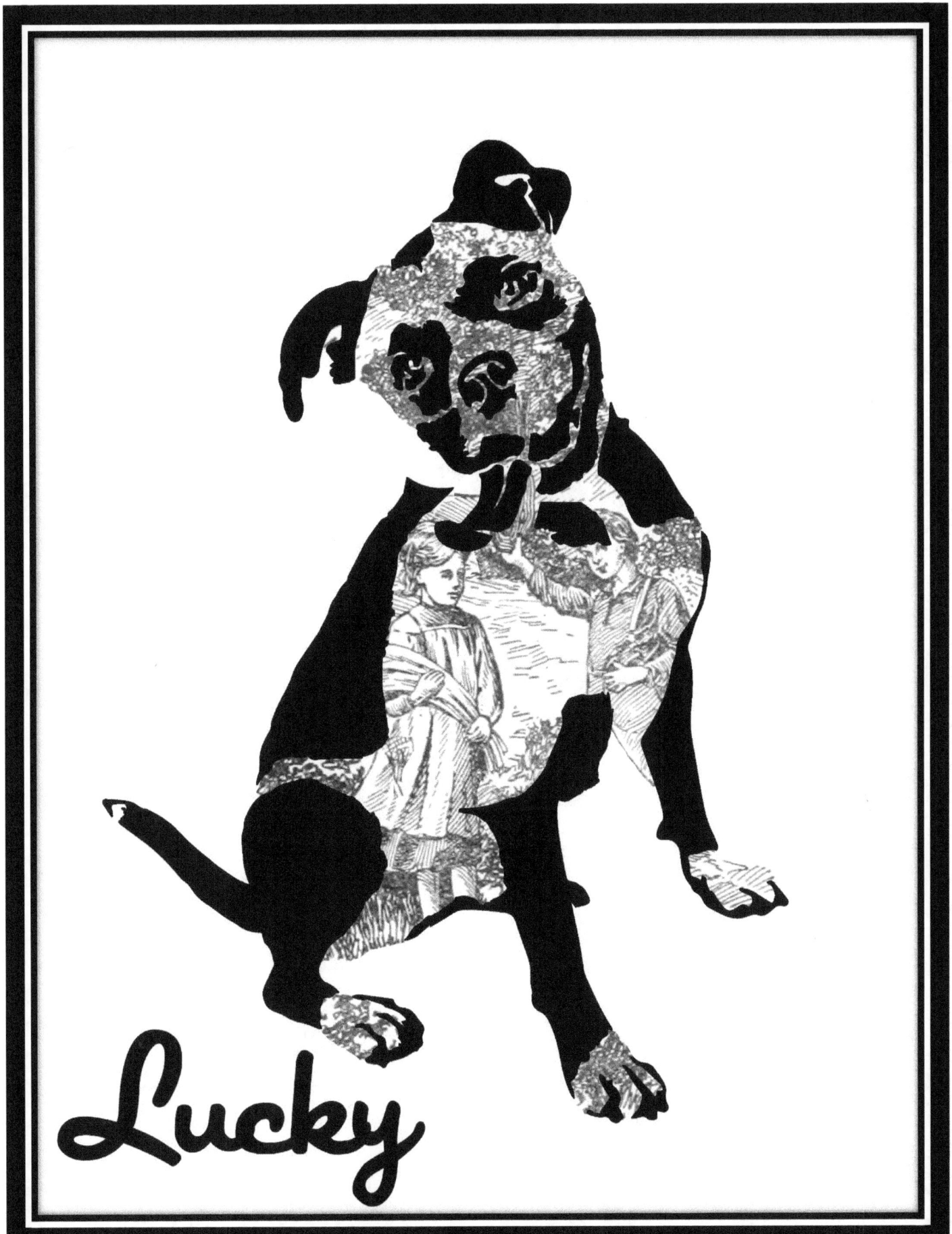

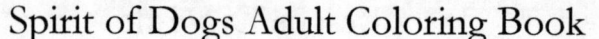

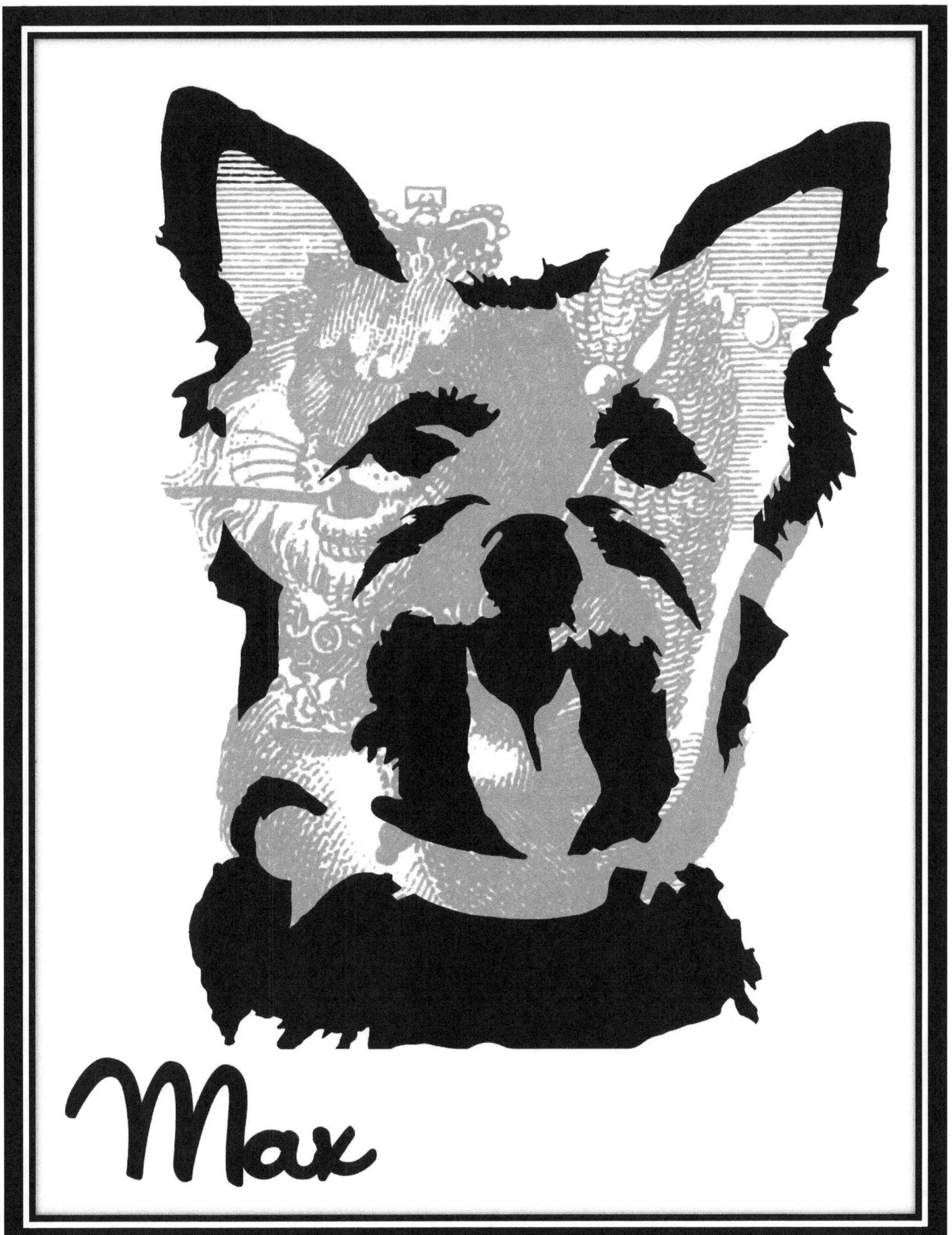

Max

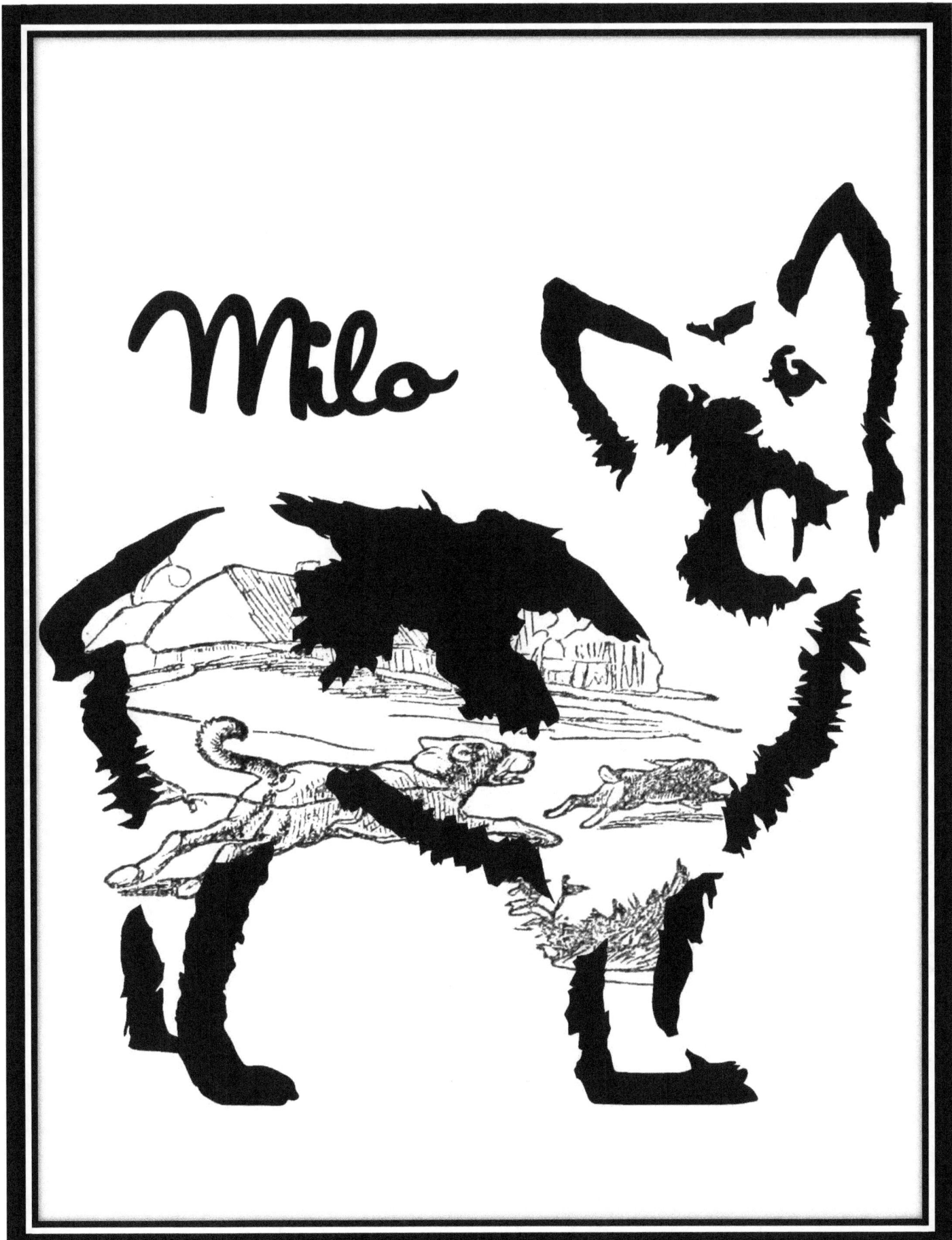

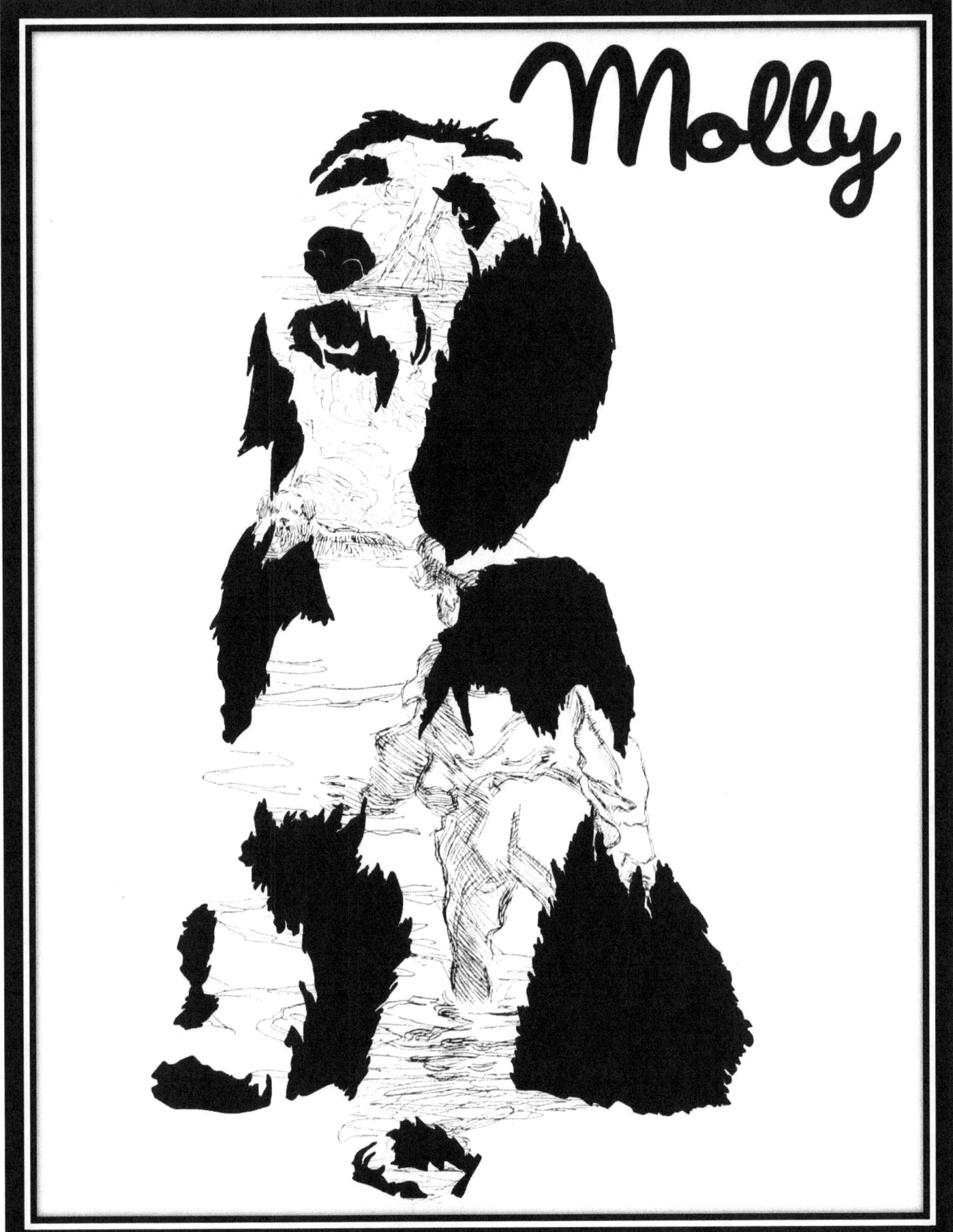

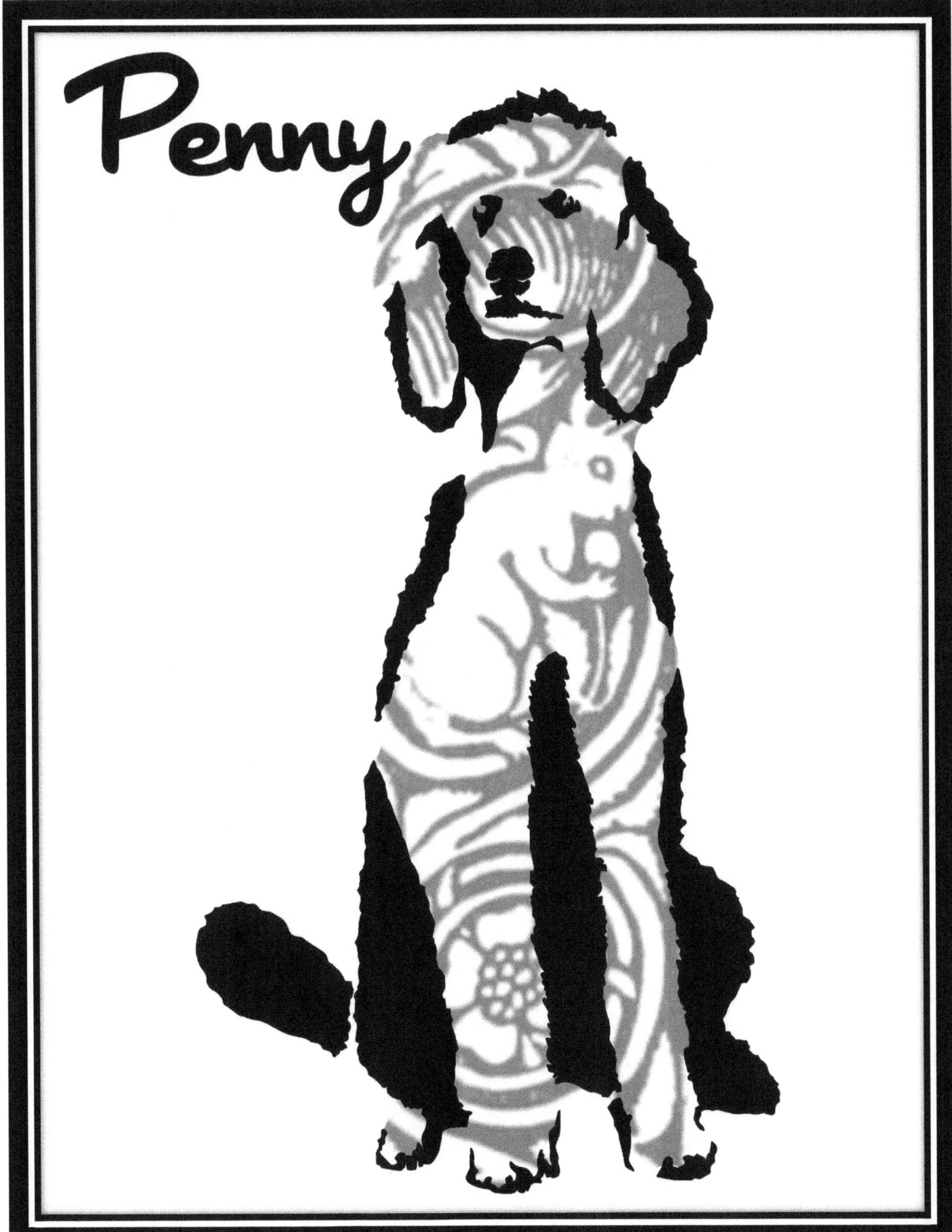

Penny

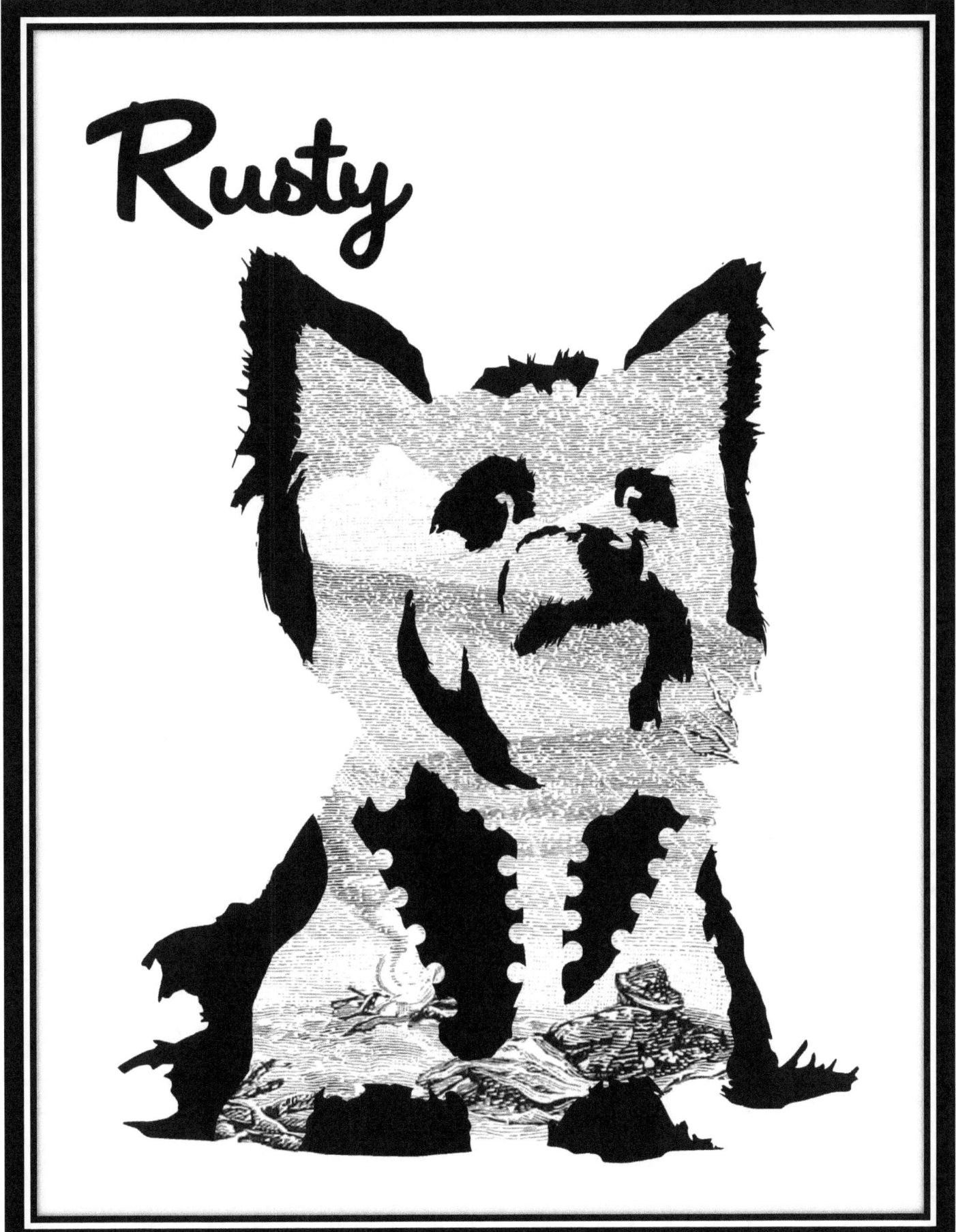

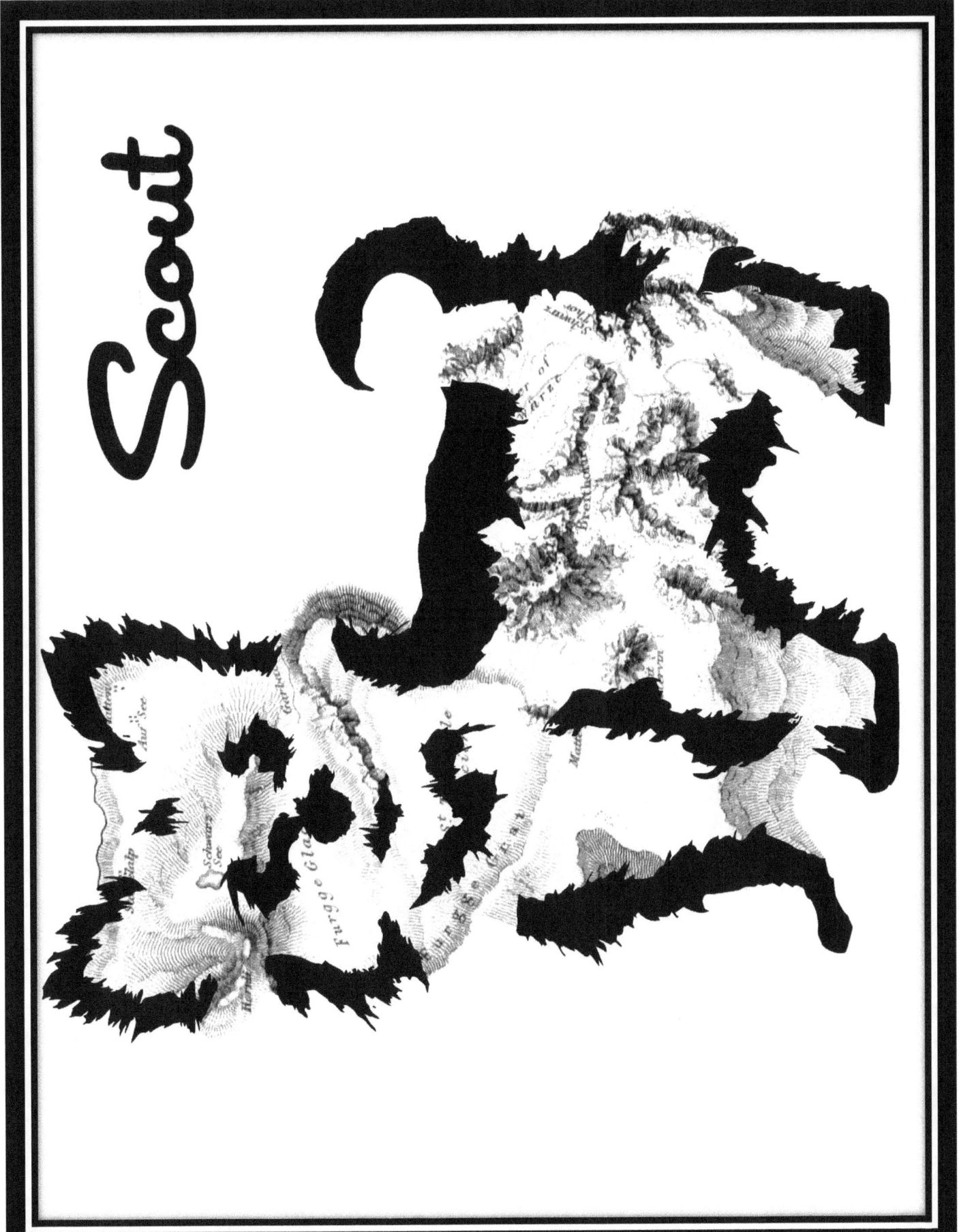

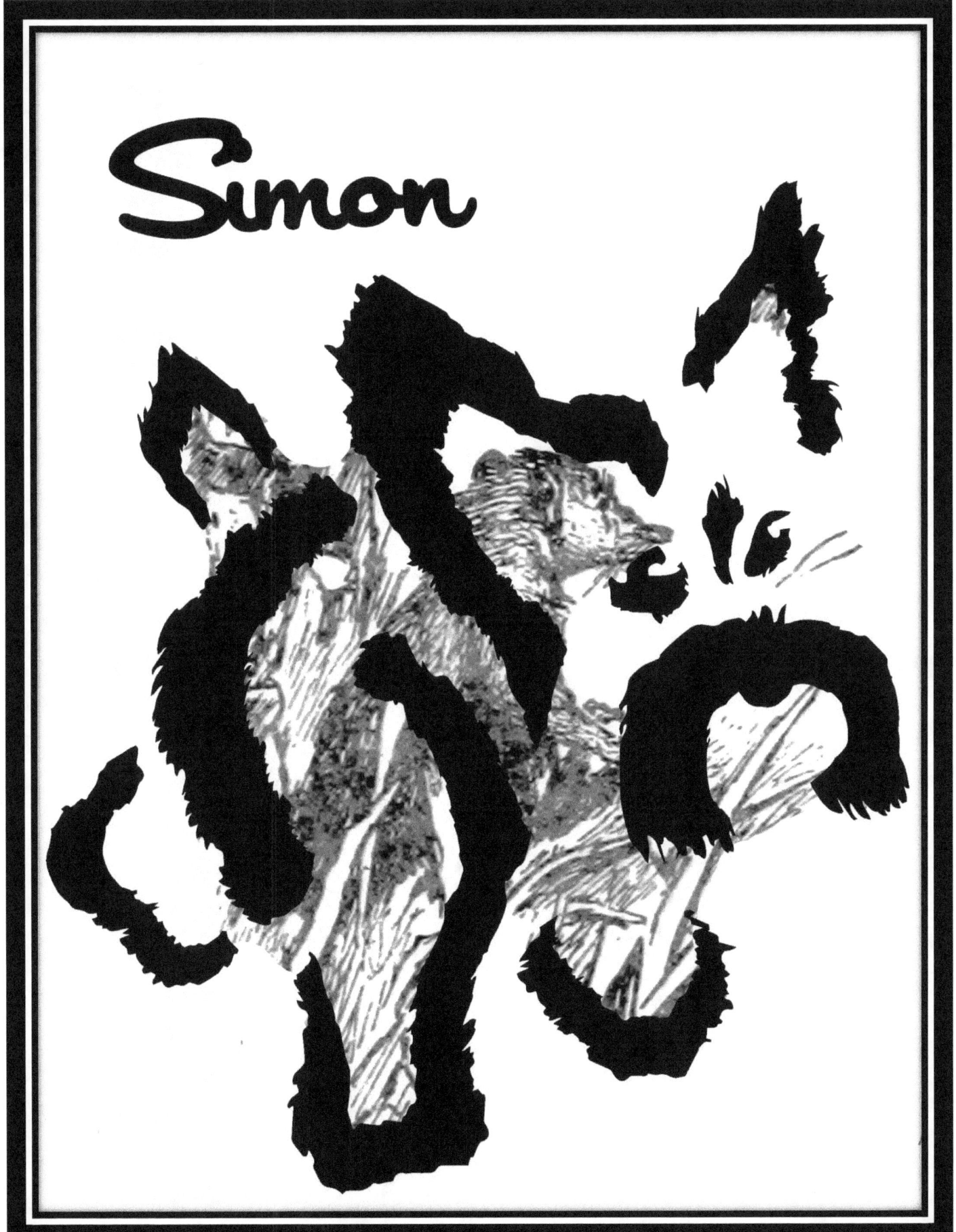

Simon

BIBLIOGRAPHY

Alpine Club London, & Ball, J. (1859). *Peaks, Passes, and Glaciers. A series of excursions by members of the Alpine Club. Edited by J. Ball. [With plates and plans.]* (monographic ed.). London: Longman & Co. Retrieved August 19, 2015, from https://flic.kr/p/hR5Ldx

Ball, N. (1891). *The pioneers of '49. A history of the excursion of the Society of California pioneers of New England.* Boston: Lee and Shepard. Retrieved August 19, 2015, from https://flic.kr/p/oujVou

Bass, F. (1900). *Stories of pioneer life, for young readers;.* Boston: D.C. Heath & Co. Retrieved November 1, 2015, from https://flic.kr/p/oeu8M2

Childs, J. L., & Collection, H. G. (1914). *Childs' Rare Flowers, Ffruits and Vegetables.* Floral Park, New York: John Lewis Childs. Retrieved August 19, 2015, from https://flic.kr/p/x7zYkp

Dodge, M. M. (1873). *St. Nicholas [serial].* New York: Scribner & Co. Retrieved November 1, 2015, from https://flic.kr/p/owc7U5

Elton, (. (1854). *The Ball of Yarn.* New York: P. J. Cozans. Retrieved August 19, 2015, from https://flic.kr/p/owduBo

Figuier, L., & Gillmore, P. (1869). *Reptiles and birds : a popular account of the various orders; with a description of the habits and economy of the most interesting.* Springfield, Mass: W.J. Holland. Retrieved November 1, 2015, from https://flic.kr/p/ot2igK

Herbert, H. W. (1868). *The complete manual for young sportsmen: with directions for handling the gun, the rifle, and the rod; the art of shooting on the wing; the breaking, management, and hunting of the dog; the varieties and habits of game; river, lake, and seafishing, etc. .* New York: W.A. Townsend & Adams. Retrieved November 1, 2015, from https://flic.kr/p/wFuUx9

Hood, T., & Shepherd, R. H. (1881). *The choice works of Thomas Hood, in prose and verse.* New York: J. W. Lovell. Retrieved November 1, 2015, from https://flic.kr/p/of2fnT

Hooker, W. J. (1830-1833). *Botanical Miscellany.* London: J. Murray. Retrieved August 19, 2015, from https://flic.kr/p/w8NLeb

Kipling, R., & Willeumier, G. (1895). *Van dieren en kinderen. Vertaling van Mevrouw Willeumier. Met platen. [Seven tales from "The Jungle Book" and "Wee Willie Winkie."]", "Selections.* Amsterdam. Retrieved August 19, 2015, from https://flic.kr/p/idMotW

Ricci, L. H., & Sara Anderson Galleries, Inc. (1915). *Illustrated catalogue of rare and beautiful Sixteenth and Seventeenth century laces collected during twenty years by Leone Ricci, Esq. of Florence.* New York: Metropolitan Art Association. Retrieved August 19, 2015, from https://flic.kr/p/od6CgP

Snyder, F. R. (n.d.). Photographs of Frank R. Snyder. *McGuffey Reader illustration.* Miami Universty LIbraries, Oxford, Ohio. Retrieved October 31, 2015, from https://flic.kr/p/5S8fmb

The Craftsman. (1901). New York: [etc]. Retrieved November 1, 2015, from https://flic.kr/p/oeSPCv

various. (1902). *Harper's New Monthly Magazine Volume 104 December 1901 to May 1902* (Vol. 104). New York: Harper & Brothers Publishers. Retrieved November 1, 2015, from https://flic.kr/p/oeSN58

W, B., & Mulready, W. (1883). *The Elephant's Ball and Grand Fete Champetre. [In verse.] Intended as companion to those much admired pieces, The Butterfly's Ball, and The Peacock "at home." Illustrated with elegant engravings [by William Mulready].* ([Another edition.] A facsimile reproduction of the edition of 1807. With an introduction by Charles Welsh. ed.). London: Griffith & Farran. Retrieved August 19, 2015, from https://flic.kr/p/ic86Qp

Ward, J., & Griffith, F. L. (1902). *The sacred beetle: a popular treatise on Egyptian scarabs in art and history.* London: J. Murray. Retrieved October 31, 2015, from https://flic.kr/p/odyhp1

Washburn & Co, & Henry G. Gilbert Nursery and Seed Trade Catalog Co. (1869). *Washburn & Co.'s amateur cultivator's guide to the flower and kitchen garden : containing a descriptive list of two thousand varieties of flower and vegetable seeds : also a list of French hybrid gladiolus,.* Boston: The Company. Retrieved Augsut 19, 2015, from https://flic.kr/p/oeRZtT

It's a Rescue Dog Life

IT'S A RESCUE DOG LIFE

It's a Rescue Dog Life is a community of Dog Lovers big and small.

Join us on our
Website www.itsarescuedoglife.com,
Facebook http://facebook.com/itsarescuedoglife